Space Explorer

THE SUN

Patricia Whitehouse

Heinemann
LIBRARY

Young
Explorer

www.heinemann.co.uk/library
Visit our website to find out more information about *Heinemann Library* books.

To order:
 Phone ++44 (0)1865 888066
 Send a fax to ++44 (0)1865 314091
 Visit the Heinemann Bookshop at **www.heinemann.co.uk/library** to browse our catalogue and order online.

First published in Great Britain by Heinemann Library, Halley Court, Jordan Hill, Oxford OX2 8EJ, part of Harcourt Education. Heinemann is a registered trademark of Harcourt Education Ltd.

Editorial: Jilly Attwood and Kate Bellamy
Design: Ron Kamen and Paul Davies
Picture Research: Ruth Blair and Sally Claxton
Production: Séverine Ribierre
Originated by Dot Gradations
Printed and bound in China by South China Printing Company

The paper used to print this book comes from sustainable resources.

ISBN 0 431 11340 8
08 07 06 05 04
10 9 8 7 6 5 4 3 2 1

British Library Cataloguing in Publication Data
Whitehouse, Patricia
The Sun – (Space Explorer)
523.7
A full catalogue record for this book is available from the British Library.

Acknowledgements
The Publishers are grateful to the following for permission to reproduce photographs: Corbis pp. **8**, **9**, **10**, **15**, **24** (royalty free); Getty Images/Photodisc pp. **5** (Photolink), **12**, **17**, **22**, **27**, **28**, **29** (Stock Trek); KPT Power Photos p. **4**; NASA p. **14**; NSO/Aura/NSF p. **16**; Science Photo Library pp. **25** (SOHO/ESA/NASA), **26** (David Nunuk); Science Photo Library pp. **13** (National Optical Astronomy Observatories), **20** (NASA)

Cover photo reproduced with permission of NASA.

Our thanks to Stuart Clark for his assistance in the preparation of this book.

Every effort has been made to contact copyright holders of any material reproduced in this book. Any omissions will be rectified in subsequent printings if notice is given to the Publishers.

Contents

Never look directly at the Sun. Its strong light could damage your eyes.

Words written in bold, **like this,** are explained in the Glossary.

 Find out more about space at www.heinemannexplore.co.uk.

What is the Sun?

The Sun is the brightest thing in the sky. It is a huge ball of hot **gases** that gives off heat and light.

Every day, people can look to the sky and see the brightness of the Sun.

On a clear night, millions of stars can be seen in the sky from Earth.

The Sun is a star, just like the stars that you can see at night. The Sun looks different because it is much closer to the Earth than the other stars.

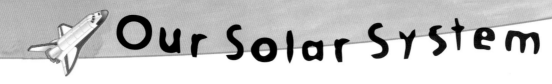

The Sun is in the centre of our **Solar System**. Solar comes from Sol, a word meaning Sun. The Earth and the other planets in the Solar System **orbit** the Sun.

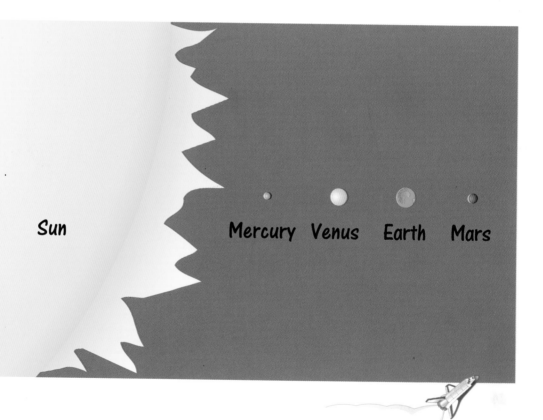

Sun   Mercury Venus Earth Mars

The first four planets in our Solar System orbit the Sun in this order.

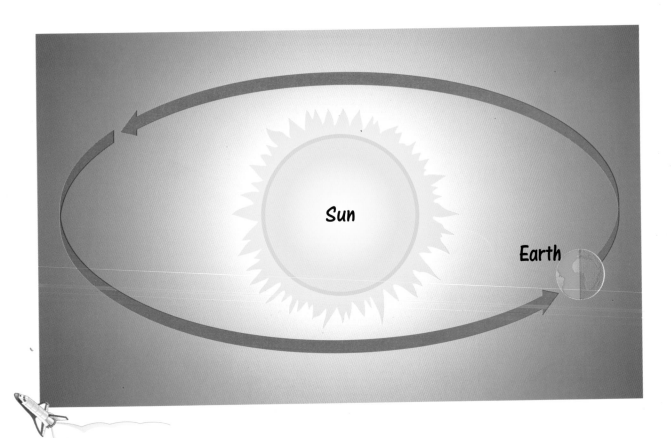

The Earth spins as it moves around the Sun.

The Earth is about 150 million kilometres from the Sun. It takes 365 days for the Earth to travel once around the Sun.

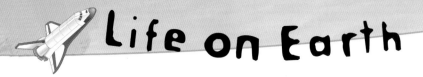

Life on Earth

The heat from the Sun helps to make the Earth warm enough for plants and animals. Plants use the Sun's light to make their food.

Animals eat plants to get the food they need to live and grow. Most living things on Earth need the Sun for life.

This deer eats green leaves and grass, which need the Sun to grow.

9

The Sun's size

From the Earth, the Sun looks like it is about the size of your thumb. It appears that size because it is so far away.

Sun

Earth

Compared to the Earth, the Sun is huge!
It would take more than 100 Earths to
form a line across the Sun. More than
one million Earths could fit inside it.

Hot gases

The Sun is a huge ball of **gases**.
It is mostly made of two gases called
hydrogen and helium. These gases
are also found on the Earth.

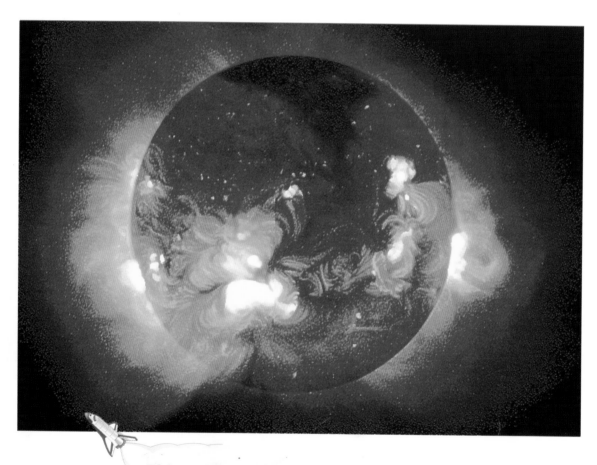

This x-ray photograph of the Sun
shows the areas that are very active.

Even though the Sun is made of gases, it is very heavy. The Sun weighs much more than all the planets and moons in the Solar System put together.

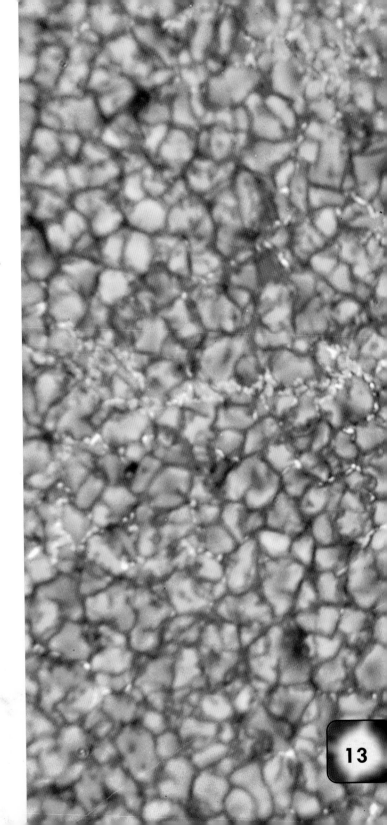

This is the surface of the Sun. The bright parts are hot gases that rise from the Sun's surface. The darker lines are cooler gases.

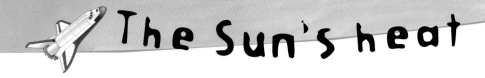

The Sun's heat

The Sun does not burn in the same way that a fire burns. The **gases** that make up the Sun are so hot that they glow.

The Sun glows even when it is setting.

In the middle of the Sun, gas is squeezed together so much that tiny parts of different gases join up. This makes powerful **nuclear energy**. Nuclear energy makes the Sun so hot.

People have learned how to use nuclear energy on Earth. Nuclear power plants make electricity and heat energy.

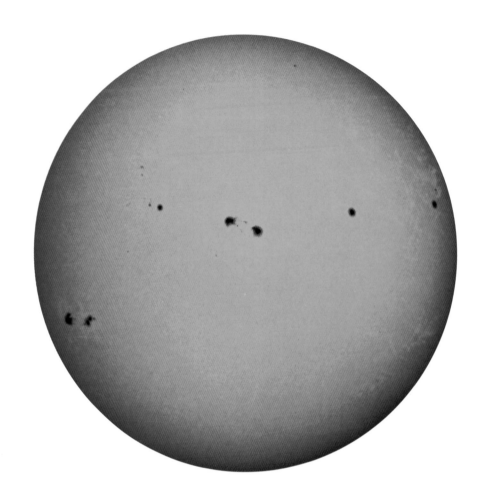

The Sun has different parts. The centre of the Sun is called the **core**. This is where **nuclear energy** is made. The bright edge of the Sun is what we can see. It is called the **photosphere**.

The **corona** is a very large area of hot **gases** that is around the Sun. It cannot always be seen, because the photosphere is so bright.

The corona can be seen when the bright photosphere is covered.

corona

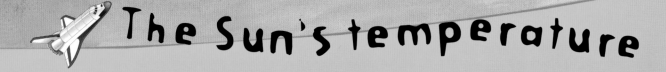

The Sun's temperature

Different parts of the Sun are hotter than other parts. The **photosphere** is about 6100°C and the **corona** can be one million °C. The Sun's **core** is 15 million °C. A very hot oven on Earth is only about 200°C.

corona 1 million °C

photosphere 6100 °C

core 15 million °C

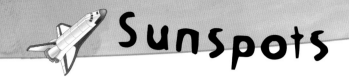

Sunspots

Sunspots are dark patches on the **photosphere**. Some are thousands of kilometres wide. Sunspots move across the photosphere. They go after a few weeks.

sunspots

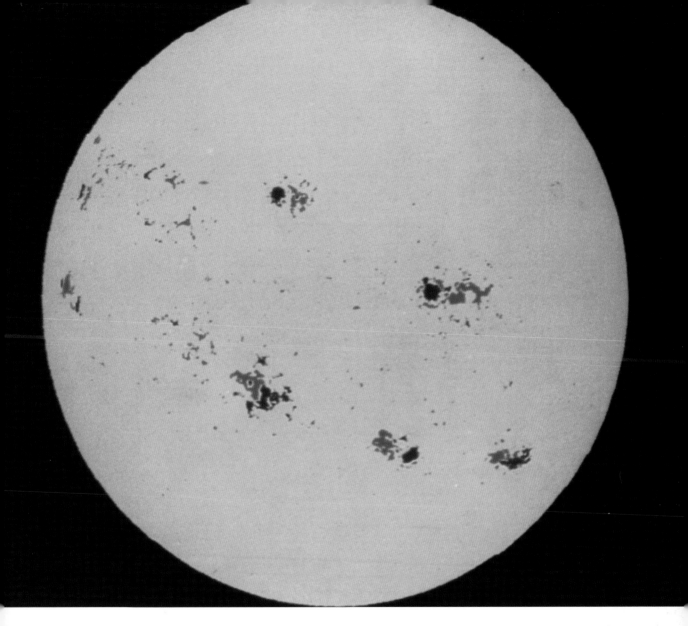

Sunspots are dark because they
are cooler than the rest of the Sun.
They don't glow as brightly as the
rest of the photosphere.

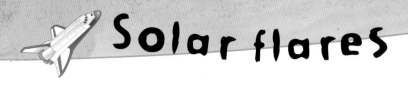

Solar flares

Solar flares are hot **gases** that explode from the **photosphere**. Some solar flares can send gases hundreds of millions of kilometres into space.

The explosion on the left of the Sun is a solar flare.

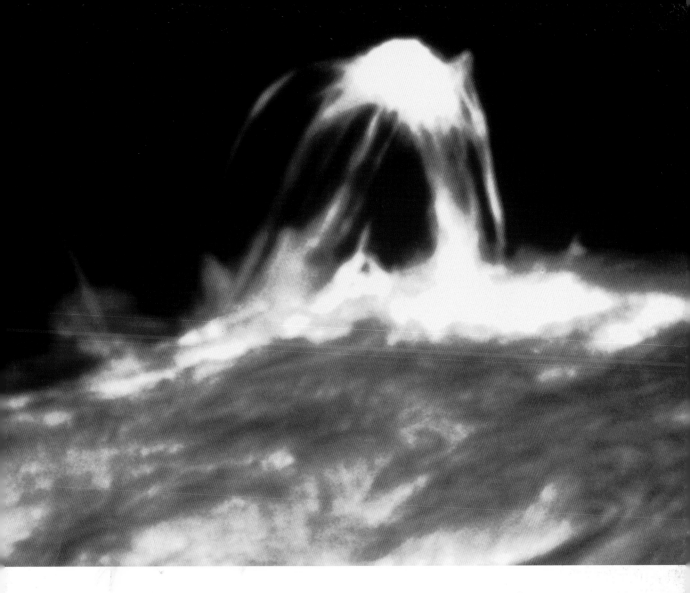

Solar flares happen during **magnetic storms** on the Sun. Each solar flare can last from a few minutes to a few hours. Some scientists think they cause giant sunquakes, a bit like earthquakes!

23

Prominences are sheets of **gas** that also begin on the **photosphere**. Prominences are much larger than **solar flares** and can last for weeks or months.

This is a large solar prominence.

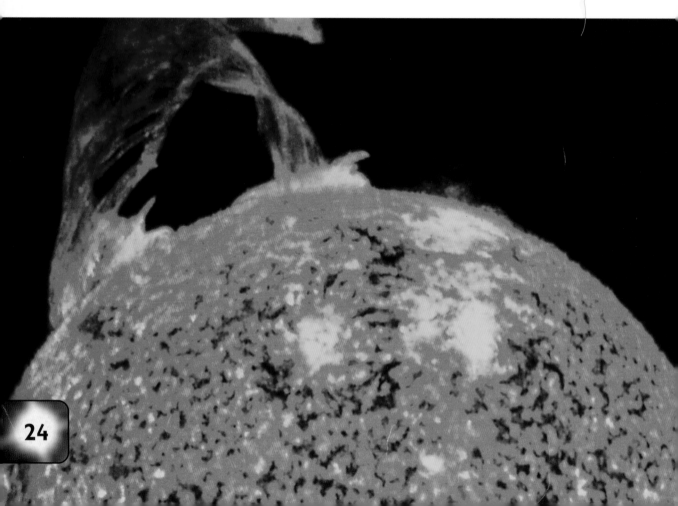

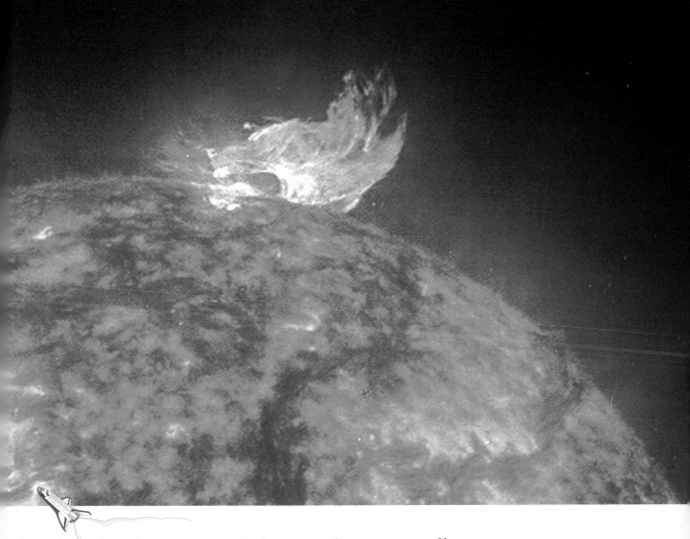

The lower part of the prominence usually falls back into the Sun.

Some prominences reach across the Sun and then fall back into the photosphere. Others carry the gases away from the Sun and into space.

Eclipses

A solar **eclipse** happens when the Moon covers the Sun's **photosphere**. For this to happen, the Moon has to be exactly between the Sun and the Earth.

The Moon is almost covering the Sun. Some people think that this stage of an eclipse looks like a diamond ring.

Sun

Sunlight

The Sun's **corona** can be
seen during an eclipse.

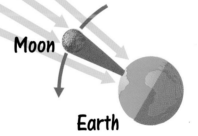

Moon

Earth

The Moon gets in the way of light
coming from the Sun. This makes
a shadow of the Moon, on the
Earth. The places on the Earth below
the shadow get dark. Other places
on the Earth stay sunny.

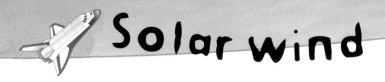

Solar wind

The Sun also gives out tiny **particles** that stream into space. These particles are called the solar wind.

This is what the solar wind looks like when it reaches Earth.

The northern lights are usually green or blue in colour.

When the solar wind reaches the Earth, it can make beautiful light patterns in the sky. The lights near the North Pole are called the northern lights. Near the South Pole they are called the southern lights.

Amazing Sun facts

- Astronomers think the Sun is about 4.6 billion years old.

- In the north, when it is summer the Sun does not set over the North Pole. This happens in the south, too.

- The longest time a solar **eclipse** can last is 7.5 minutes.

- The Sun is 700 times bigger than all the planets of the Solar System put together.

Find out more about space at www.heinemannexplore.co.uk.

Glossary

core the centre section of the Sun

corona part of the Sun

eclipse when an object in space blocks the light from the Sun

gas air-like material that is not solid or liquid

magnetic storms storms on the Sun caused by magnetic forces

nuclear energy when different parts of a gas join together to make powerful energy

orbit path one object makes around another

particles very small bits of matter

photosphere the outer part of the Sun

prominences sheets of gas from the Sun

solar flare hot gases that explode from the Sun's photosphere

Solar System the Sun and everything that orbits it, including the nine planets and their moons

More books and websites

The Earth (Space Explorer), P. Whitehouse (Heinemann Library, 2004)
The Moon (Space Explorer), P. Whitehouse (Heinemann Library, 2004)
The Planets (Space Explorer), P. Whitehouse (Heinemann Library, 2004)
The Stars (Space Explorer), P. Whitehouse (Heinemann Library, 2004)

www.esa.int
www.nasa.gov/audience/for kids

Index

Titles in the *Space Explorer* series include:

Hardback   0 431 11347 5

Hardback   0 431 11348 3

Hardback   0 431 11345 9

Hardback   0 431 11342 4

Hardback   0 431 11341 6

Hardback   0 431 11344 0

Hardback   0 431 11343 2

Hardback   0 431 11340 8

Hardback   0 431 11346 7

Find out about the other titles in this series on our website www.heinemann.co.uk/library